HOW TO WRITE

A

RESEARCH

MANUSCRIPT

IN 1 WEEK

CHAPTER ONE

INTRODUCTION

This book explain in simple and practical way how researchers can write their manuscript in one week. It is designed for beginners and researchers who do not have experience in writing and publications.

Research final products can include many such as thesis, dissertation, conference paper and manuscript.

Manuscript is small and brief summary of the research findings and sometimes can produce more the one manuscript for each research project.

Most scientific journals use the following design for original research manuscript:

<u>IMRAD Format</u>

- Introduction
- Methods
- Results
- And
- Discussion

❖   What you need

To start writing your research manuscript you need the following items to be ready before starting:

- Objectives of the research

- Methods (including data collection)

- Data analysed

- Literature review

All the above can be in draft version

The most important parts of any manuscript are

❖ Abstract

❖ Tables & Figures

❖ Conclusions

CHAPTER TWO

Day 1

WRITE THE METHODS

We start writing the methods as first part of the manuscript because the study already finished and data collection done. All methods details been discussed and approved prior to data collection. It's usually 200-400 words.

Methods part usually consist of :

- ❖ Study design
- ❖ Study population
- ❖ Sampling methods
- ❖ Data collection

- ❖ Study tools

- ❖ Ethical consideration

- ❖ Statistical analysis

- ❖ Variables definition

- Methods is the technical part of the manuscript

- Usually reviewers check this part first to see if the study conducted in correct and clear manner.

You need to focus on following points :

❖ *Describe study population and location*

o Put in details the location of the study, the inclusion and exclusion criteria for the population

❖ *Study design*

o Need to mention whether it is observational or experimental

o If experimental need to explain in detail the protocol, randomization, blinding even registration of the trial.

❖ *Study tools*

o Mention about tools used like blood taking, blood pressure measurement, weight and height measurement and put in details the brand name of the tool

❖ *List of questionnaires used and from where adopted?*

It is very important to mention if the questionnaires used in your study was

▪ Adopted

If adopted from previous research need to put the reference of the questionnaires and off course approval to reuse it.

▪ Modified

If taken from multiple research and modified to suit your local population, you need to show the validation process

- Newley developed

If this is the first time these questions been used. Need to show in detail the development process of the questionnaires and also pretest and pilot study results.

❖ *Any pretest done? Validation?*

You need to show the details and calculation for pretest and pilot study if the questionnaires were modified. You need to mention reliability test value (Cronbach's alpha), validity and factor analysis

❖ *Sampling methods*

How did you collect your sample, either using non-probability or probability sampling methods?

❖   *State ethics approval from which institute*

It's very important to mention ethics approval and from which institute was obtain whether university, hospital or ministry and that all participants sign the consent form and an explanation done to then regarding the study (risks, benefits, confidentiality).

Even animal studies need ethical approval.

Nowadays some journal will ask to upload a copy of ethics committee approval and approval number.

❖   *Statistics analysis software used*

Need to mention the statistical software used to analyze the data such as SPSS, STAT, R, JASP and many more. Preferably put reference to your statistical software.

❖   *What test you used and type of your study variables*

Need to mention statistical test used like for descriptive (mean and standard deviation) or frequency and percentage for numerical data. Inferential statistics like t test, chi square and ANOVA. If you have multivariable analysis like logistic regression need to put which variable was the reference, the model R square and method used.

Definition of the variables must be included especially for scale (need to mention maximum score and cut off points) . it is about how the variable was measured in the current study.

Methods

A cross-sectional survey was conducted among children aged 7–8 years from five different primary schools in Baghdad City during September–October, 2011. Questionnaires were used to assess the living environment and IQ was assessed using standardized measures. Self-administered questionnaires were distributed to the participating children's parents.

A list of all schools in the city of Baghdad was obtained from the Ministry of Education. Baghdad is divided into five educational areas, and one school was selected from each of them. Simple random sampling was used to select the five schools. The five educational areas represent people living a range of conditions, and include of both high and low socio-economic groups.

From each selected school, a complete list of student names was obtained. Stratified random sampling according to grade was then used to identify 106 children from each school. To avoid a possible influence of puberty on the measures of interest, children aged 7–8 years were selected as the study population.

The Raven's Colored Progressive Matrices (CPM) test was used to obtain child IQ score, with a maximum total score of 36 points. The test consists of 36 items in three sets of 12: A, AB and B. It is designed for use with young children for anthropological studies and for clinical work. It can be used with people who for any reason cannot speak the English language [10]. Any score higher than the 75th percentile is considered to indicate

The living environment was defined as the place where the child's family is living. An insecure living environment was defined as lacking a sense of security or affording no ease or reassurance, wherein the living situation is threatened. The living environment questionnaire consists of three domains: physical safety (hearing any gun shots or explosions, or seeing dead bodies), mental stress (worrying about child safety, child witnessing any type of explosion, thinking of leaving the house and relocating to a different area, thinking the living area is insecure), and public services (water quality, hours of electricity supply).

The questionnaire consists of 13 items, each with three response options: never (2), Occasionally (1) and Frequently (0). The maximum total score was 26. A score of 13 was taken as the cut-point because if the respondents were to answer 'most of the time' for all questions, the total score is 13. Any score less than 13 indicated a poor living environment, whereas a score above 13 indicated a good living environment.

A pilot test of the questionnaires was carried out among 31 parents. Back-to-back translation was conducted to validate the questionnaires in Arabic language. Face validity was also tested. The living environment scale had a good internal consistency, with a Cronbach's alpha coefficient of 0.827.

The study was approved by the Research and Ethics Committee of the Universiti Kebangsaan Malaysia Medical Centre. Also approval from Iraqi ministry of education was obtained to conduct the research inside the schools.

and for family income was high. All analyses were performed using SPSS version 16.0 [12].

Statistical analysis

The association between child IQ status and living environment status (good/poor) was examined by a Chi
squared test (for categorical variables). A logistic regression analysis was conducted to determine the factors
associated with IQ status. Odds ratios were obtained for
each potential factor after adjustment for age, sex, school
grade, family income and parent education level. The
mental stress, physical safety and public services domains were treated as continuous variables. The reference for gender was male, for educational level was high,

CHAPTER THREE

Day 2

Write tables and figures

Next to write is the tables and figure because we already analysed the data before we start writing the manuscript.

General rules for tables:

- Maximum of 4-5 tables

- Title of each table must be self-explanatory

- Table should not be large (maximum 6 columns and 12 rows)

- Include confidence interval and p value where possible

The common sequence of tables as follow:

- Table 1: Socio-demographic characteristics

- Table 2: Dependent variable (outcome)

- Table 3: Association table (Socio-demographic and dependent)

- Table 4: Association table (other factors and dependent)

- Table 5: Multivariable table

Table 1: Socio-demographic characteristics of the respondents

Variables	Frequency	%
Gender		
Male	206	39.8
Female	312	60.2
Race		
Malay	388	74.9
Chinese	39	7.5
Indian	64	12.4
Other	27	5.2
Working status		
Yes	309	59.7
No	209	40.3
Family history		
Hypertension	242	46.7
Diabetes mellitus	240	46.3
Heart disease	103	19.9
Cancer	63	12.2
Stress levels		
Normal	360	69.5
Mild	75	14.5
Moderate	47	9.1
Severe	26	5.0
Extremely severe	10	1.9
Eating self-regulatory skills		
Low level	56	10.8
Medium	337	65.1
High	125	24.1

Example on descriptive table for categorical variables Need to put frequency and percentage

Table 2: Blood pressure, glucose and anthropometric measurement

Reading	Minimum	Maximum	Mean	Standard deviation
Systolic BP (mmHg)	76.00	206.00	128.16	19.641
Diastolic BP (mmHg)	48.00	130.00	80.32	10.66
Heart rate (bpm)	39.00	125.00	80.40	12.14
Blood sugar (mmol L^{-1})	2.00	31.60	7.29	3.652
Weight (kg)	38.40	132.20	68.54	16.03
Height (cm)	116.50	186.00	159.54	8.48
BMI	14.34	52.29	26.87	5.67

Example on Descriptive table for Numerical variables

❖ **Need to put Mean & SD for normally distributed variables**

❖ **Put median and IQR for not normally distributed variables**

Table 6: Association between dietary habits (SREBQ) with hypertension and diabetes

Variables	Hypertension, n (%)		X^2 (df)	p-value
	Yes	No		
Eating habits score				
Low	7 (12.5)	49 (87.5)	1.998	0.368
Medium	57 (16.9)	280 (83.1)		
High	26 (20.8)	99 (79.2)		
	Diabetes mellitus, n (%)			
	Yes	No		
Eating habits score				
Low	5 (8.9)	51 (91.1)	1.061	0.588
Medium	42 (12.5)	295 (87.5)		
High	18 (14.4)	107 (85.6)		

*Level of significance at $p < 0.05$, Chi-square test was performed

Table 4: Association between body composition variables and diabetes mellitus status

Variables	Diabetes		p-value	95% CI
	No diabetic	Diabetic		
	Mean $\pm$ SD			
Body fat (%)	31.6842±12.94869	35.0545±11.87660	0.004	-5.66581 to -1.07486
Muscle mass	43.2789±9.81210	44.0710±10.44750	0.395	-2.62041 to 1.03626
Body water (%)	49.6184±8.48435	48.2420±8.05835	0.076	-0.14400 to 2.89675
Bone mass (kg)	2.5367±0.47818	2.5556±0.49661	0.674	-0.10723 to 0.06937
Visceral fat	8.4447±4.68089	10.6591±5.30851	<0.001	-3.10787 to -1.32083
Basal metabolic rate	1340.3129±259.06990	1355.7614±276.84506	0.530	-63.78654 to 32.88955
Metabolic age	44.2164±18.01563	52.7784±15.03564	<0.001	-11.67181 to -5.45226

*Level of significance at p<0.05, independent t-test was performed

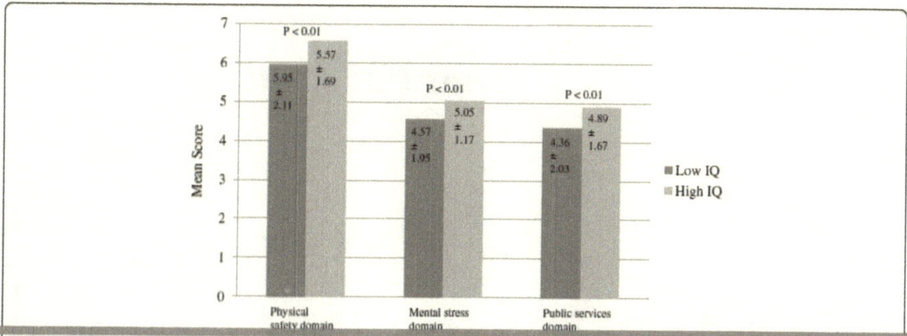

Figure 1 Association between living environment domain and child IQ status. Note: Higher scores indicate more favorable conditions. The figure represent the association between environmental domains (physical safety , mental stress and public services) with child's IQ level. The three bars represent the domains mean score in low and high IQ level groups. The values inside the bars represent mean ± standard deviation. Independent t test was performed to assess the association between the three domains and IQ and it appeared to be significant with p value of < 0.01 respectively. The higher the score of the three domains the better the IQ, in mental stress domain the higher score represent less stress, same things for the other two domains.

Figure legend to explain
what is shown

CHAPTER FOUR

Day 3

Results

- No need to explain each table in detail only headlines

- **Example:** the percentage of females were 70% and majority had university level of education as shown in table 1

So, once we put that females are 70% no need to repeat that males only 30% only mention one of them and no need to put in detail the occupation or income as readers can refer to table 1 for more information.

- Usually 500-1000 words

- First paragraph describes the characteristics of the sample

- Mention response rate if it was population study

- The tense to use in data writing is past tense

- The tense to use in referring to tables or figures should be present tense

When referring to data can use the following sentences

- As detailed in Figure 2

- In Figure. 3, we compare or present

- We observe / conclude / deduce from table 2 that

- As shown in table 1

- Table 1 represents the socio- demographic characteristics of the respondents

Results

In total, 529 children aged 7–8 years participated in the study, a response rate of 88.1% (529/600). The participants' average age was 7.99 years (SD ± 0.55). The IQ scores showed that 77.7% of the participants had a high intelligence level as they scored higher than the 75th percentile. The participants' median monthly family income was 754,901 Iraqi dinars (approximately 649USD).

Table 1 presents the participants' socio-demographic characteristics. Slightly more than half (52.2%) were male, and 80.7% had a good living environment.

Table 2 displays the number and proportion of children in each of the two IQ status groups by questionnaire item. Most of the parents (65.2%) reported that the unstable security situation in the last 8 years occasionally affected their family's daily life, while 22.9% reported that their family's daily life was frequently affected.

There were significant associations between child IQ status and seeing dead bodies in the street, child witnessing any type of explosion, problems attending school every day, child missing school because of an unstable security situation, electricity supply to the house, problems with grocery shopping, water quality and insecure living area.

Figure 1 displays the mean living environment domain scores (physical safety, mental stress and services provided to the house) by child IQ status. There were

CHAPTER FIVE

Day 4

Introduction / background

- its usually referred to as introduction or background depends on journal format

- Maximum 3-4 paragraphs

- 100-200 words to introduce your topic

- 500-1000 words of literature review

- Last paragraph should be the aim of the study (general objective)

- Usually can put up to 10 references in introduction part

Components

- History (Statistics)

- Importance

- Gaps in knowledge

Why this is a problem

- Clearly state the importance of the research

- What's new in your work

- What are your contributions to the development of the field

What?

- Problem statement and main purpose

- Describe the problem you address in the paper

Why

- Why do you address that issue?

- What applications does this research problem have?

Critical literature review

- Most relevant works / literature review (Usually 10 years duration)

- If there is any gap in knowledge

Usually introduction part cover three areas:

- ❖ What we already know

- ❖ What we do not know

- ❖ What current paper will add

Background

The consequences of war are not limited to impaired physical health. War may also impair the mental health of affected individuals. The negative consequences for mental health can be significant, especially when the victims are children. Living in an unstable environment during childhood has detrimental effects on children, especially on their cognitive development. A few studies have examined the effects of war and terrorism on child cognitive development. Joshi and Donnell [1] concluded that any war or act of terror, as a sudden, unpredictable, and dramatic event, has a tremendous negative impact

Start with brief introduction to your research topic

at various levels, including the community, family, and individual. Children are usually the most affected by these experiences. Delaney-Black [2] examined the relationship between violence exposure, trauma-related distress and standardized test performance among 299 urban first-grade children and their caregivers. Exposure to violence affected the child's IQ and reading ability. A child experiencing exposure to violence and trauma-related distress at or above the 90th percentile would be expected to have a 7.5 point decrement in IQ and a 9.8 point decrement in reading achievement. Delaney-Black concluded that for young children, exposure to violence and trauma-related distress was associated with substantial decrements in IQ and reading achievement.

During the past three decades, the health of Iraqi people has substantially deteriorated. Since 1980, the country has been caught up in a continuous wave of war

last paragraph of the introduction must be aim or objectives of the study

> This aim of this study was to assess the effect of living in an insecure environment on child intelligence quotients (IQ). We focused on the effects of living in an unstable security situation on the mental health and physical safety of household members and the services provided to the house.

CHAPTER SIX

Day 5

Discussion

General rules:

- Usually consist of 3-4 paragraphs

- The range of words count between 500-1000 words

- 1ST paragraph about the study main findings

- 2ND paragraph regarding the study limitations

- 3RD and 4th paragraph: compare your results with previous studies.

Important issue to consider when writing discussion

- Need to evaluate the data and discuss their importance

- Focus on the main findings

- Justify any assumptions you make

- Consider and discuss alternative explanations

- Agreement or disagreement with other studies

- If your findings contradicted with previous findings need to give explanation

Modal verbs in discussion

- Modal verbs are important in the discussion part

- The most commonly used modal verbs in science writing are:

<u>may, might, could, can, should, ought to, need to, have to, must</u>

❖ Example:

The drop in volume **<u>was</u>** due to a loss of fluid (states the definite reason)

The correct

The drop in volume **<u>may have been</u>** due to a loss of fluid (suggests a possible reason)

Discussion

The mental stress and public service domains were the two most important living environment conditions affecting child IQ in Baghdad, Iraq. The physical safety domain was not associated with child IQ. Monthly family income was significantly associated with child IQ, which is in agreement with a number of studies that report significant effects of poverty on children's cognitive and verbal skills [13-15]. Low income results in less food and nutrients for the child, which will in turn affect their development. In this study, parent education level was not associated with child IQ status, although other studies have found a significant relationship between parent education level and child IQ [16]. The majority of the parents in our study area had a high education level, which may explain this discrepancy.

More than two-thirds of the children's parents were found to live in a good environment according to our cut-off point. The Centre for Strategic and International Studies [17] stated in their 2010 report that "There are a wide range of indicators that show the level of violence in Iraq has dropped sharply since the 2006 year, the average number of security incidents between September and November 2009 was only half that of the same period in 2008." In addition, the Oxford Research Group Security Report [18] concluded that most of the available evidence supports the view that security within Iraq has substantially improved, but there is still endemic violence, especially in the capital city of Baghdad.

Mental stress domain scores were correlated with child IQ, suggesting that exposure to mental stress is detrimental to child IQ. The two most important components of this domain were child witnessing any type of explosion and insecure family living area in which they perceive as movement restriction and lacking of daily living needs. According other studies [19,20], intensive and continuous exposure to multiple stressful events in conflict and disaster settings is a major risk factor for negative mental health consequences for children and adolescents. Additionally, Tol et al. [21] noted that exposure to violence is a risk factor for adverse child development outcomes in low-income settings, and that childhood mental health problems are difficult to address within the context of ongoing poverty and political instability.

The services domain, which relates to electricity supply to the house, water quality and problems grocery shopping, was also associated with child IQ. It is already established by previous research [22-24] that the quality of the home environment accounts for significant variance in child academic outcomes. In this study, the physical safety domain was not associated with child IQ. A possible reason for this is the improvement in the security situation in Baghdad, because the numbers of dead bodies on the streets, gun

Compare with previous research

There are few limitations can be identified in this study; involvement of male is '0' due to minimal number of them work in ETD where the respondents have been chosen randomly and none of them works at health clinics, therefore researcher could not make a comparison and obtain the association with the gender. Also, short working experience of 2 months is too short and at least a 1-year experience should be included in future researches.

Study Limitations

CHAPTER SEVEN

Day 6

Conclusion & references

- ❖ **Conclusion**

- Usually less than 200 words

- Consist of 1 paragraph and maximum 3-4 sentences

- Some journals format can include recommendations with conclusion

- Give recommendations for future studies

Tips for writing conclusion

- Try to include your own views

- It's ok to write a short conclusion of 1-2 sentences

- Put in your mind that readers have already read the full paper and make their views about your research and findings.

Conclusions

In Iraq, child IQ was found to be associated with the mental stress and public service domains of the living environment. We hope that our study results will help the authorities and policy makers in Iraq in their efforts to improve the living situation of Iraqis.

Brief conclusion and usually similar to conclusion part in abstract

Competing interests

The authors declare that they have no competing interests.

Must declare if any competence of interest

Authors' contributions

HFG: Conceived the study idea, analyzed the data and wrote the manuscript. ZMI: contributed to the idea and discussion. SAJ: contributed to discussion. SAS: contributed to analysis and discussion. AMT: contributed to analysis. MAQ: contributed to the methodology. All authors read and approved the final manuscript.

Some journals ask for each co-author contribution

Acknowledgments

This study was funded by the Universiti Kebangsaan Malaysia Medical Centre Fundamental Research Grant, Code Number FF-180-2011 without which the study would not have been possible. In addition, we received financial support from the United Nations University, International Institute for Global Health, Kuala Lumpur, Malaysia.

Acknowledgment is to thank people who helped in data collection

References

- Usually 20-40 maximum

- The format depends on journal format

- For electronic references like WHO need to put the URL and date of accessed

- The common reference styles are: Harvard, Vancouver and APA

- Better to use reference management software such as:

❖ RefWorks

❖ Zotero

❖ EndNote

❖ Mendeley

❖ CiteULike

	Cost	Integration with Microsoft office	Can capture webpage to create record
RefWorks	Need subscription	Yes	Yes
Zotero	Free	Yes	Yes
EndNote	Need subscription	Yes	No
Mendeley	Free	Yes	Yes
CiteULike	Free	Yes	Yes

References

1. Joshi T, O'Donnell A: **Consequences of child exposure to war and terrorism.** *Clin Child Fam Psychol Rev* 2003, 6:275–292.
2. Delaney-Black V: **Violence exposure, trauma, and IQ and/or reading deficits among urban children.** *Arch Pediatr Adolesc Med* 2002, 156:280–285.
3. Cockburn P: *The occupation, war and resistance in Iraq.* 2nd edition. London: Verso publication; 2007.
4. Steele J: *Defeat: why America and Britain Lost Iraq, I.B.* 1st edition. Great Britain: Tauris & Co Ltd; 2008.
5. UNICEF: *UNICEF/Donor Consolidated Report 2003. The revised crisis appeal.* Paris: 2003.

CHAPTER EIGHT

Day 7

Abstract

- The most important part of the Manuscript

- Most of the time when you send paper to a journal, the Editor-In-Chief will read the abstract to see if your paper can be sent to external reviewer.

- Most readers only read abstract especially, for closed access papers

- Readers use the abstract to decide whether or not to read and cite the paper

- The abstract is not an introduction to the paper

- It is a brief summary of each of the main IMRAD sections of the paper

- Brief summary of the whole paper, so that readers understand it without reading the other parts of the manuscript.

General rules

- Avoid the classical "In this paper" starting

- Avoid adding references & citation in the abstract

- Avoid acronyms or spell the full name first then put abbreviation

- There are two types of abstract (structure vs unstructured) depend on journal format

- Tense: either <u>past</u> or <u>present</u> tense may be used

Example of structure type of abstract

Abstract

Background: Environmental factors play a very important role in the child development process, especially in a situation like that of Iraq. Thirteen years of economic sanctions followed by the 2003 war and 8 years of unstable security have affected the daily life of Iraqi families and children. The objective of this study was to assess the associations between living environment domains and child intelligence quotient (IQ) score.

Methods: A cross-sectional survey was conducted among 529 children aged 7–8 years from five primary schools in Baghdad during September–October, 2011. The five schools represent people living a range of conditions, and include of both high and low socio-economic groups. Living environment was assessed by 13 questionnaire items, consists of three domains: physical safety , mental stress and public services. While IQ was assessed by Raven Colored progressive matrices.

Results: Among the participants, 22% were of low intelligence versus 77% of high intelligence and 19% lived in a poor environment. There were significant associations between the mental stress and service living environment domains and child IQ (p = 0.009 and p = 0.001, respectively).

Conclusion: In Iraq, child IQ was found to be associated with the mental stress and service domains of the living environment. This study findings will help authorities in their efforts to improve living environment.

Keywords: Baghdad City, IQ, Living environment, Primary school children

Example of unstructured type of abstract

ABSTRACT

As a front-liner in healthcare services, nurses play an important role in managing disaster victims. Thus, it is crucial for nurses to be prepared when facing disaster. The aim of this paper is to determine the knowledge of emergency nurses (EN) and community health nurses (CHN) with respect to disaster management, as well as identify predictor factors. This comparative cross-sectional study was conducted between October and November 2011. The 17-items of the self-developed questionnaire in assessing knowledge towards disaster management were distributed to randomly selected nurses from 10 emergency and trauma departments (132 respondents) and 8 health clinics (264 respondents) in one of the state in Malaysia. The results showed that both groups had a comparable median score on knowledge, 58.82 with interquartile range (IQR) =52.94-70.58 for EN and IQR=48.53-69.12 for CHN. No significant difference in knowledge was identified within these groups, with approximately 59.1% having inadequate knowledge of disaster management. Attending disaster-related education/training was identified as a predictor factor for adequacy of knowledge among EN with significant value of p<0.01, (AOR) of 3.807, 95% (CI) of 1.584-9.153) and CHN (p<0.001, AOR=3.511, 95% CI=2.097-5.881). As conclusion, emergency and community health nurses have inadequate knowledge with regard to disaster management, and it has been demonstrated statistically that adequacy of knowledge is driven by attending disaster-related education/training, which predicts knowledge level. Therefore, it is paramount for organizations to conduct disaster-related education/training to improve nurses' knowledge.

Tips to write good abstract

❖ Write the abstract after you finish writing your paper

❖ Choose main points from your introduction and conclusion

❖ Pick out key findings from the methods

❖ Pick out the major findings from results

❖ Add a sentence or two as a conclusion

❖ Don't add any new information or undefined abbreviations

❖ Do not add any references in the abstract

❖ Link your sentences so that the information flows clearly

❖ Check if points presented in your paper and abstract are consistent

❖ Ask your colleague to review your abstract and give you feedback

❖ Finally, check if your abstract meet journal format

keywords

- You must choose **3-5** keywords.

- These will decide whether your paper will be cited in the future or not.

- When academic researcher search for papers in online engines they will enter keywords so if you put the right one your paper will appear to them and they will cite your work.

- Use the same keywords that you use to find a previous papers

Title

- Usually Journals will ask for 2 titles (the full title and short running title)

- Your manuscript title can be different from your research or proposal title

Tips for good title:

- Used attractive words, put place of study and some journals will ask to put study design in the title, like cross-sectional study.

- Avoid titles with more than 20 words

- Rewrite the title in the final version of the paper

- Don't use acronyms and abbreviations in the title

- Avoid waste words (studies on, investigations on)

- Sometimes the title may contain the conclusion of the paper.

CHAPTER NINE

Summary

This simple and practical guide to write research manuscript in just 7 days only applicable if you have the research in draft version.

These steps will help and guide researchers to transfer their research findings into manuscript that can be published in peer reviewed journals.

Structure of Manuscript

<table>
<tr><td>

TITLE
(Should be less than 20 words and contain the 3<u>W</u> (What, Who, Where)

</td></tr>
</table>

<table>
<tr><td>

Author Names and Affiliations

</td></tr>
</table>

<table>
<tr><td>

ABSTRACT (less than 250 words)

- Introduction / Background (Must contain aim or objective of the study)
- Methods
- Results
- Conclusion

</td></tr>
</table>

<table>
<tr><td>

KEYWORDS

- a list of 3–5 key words is to be provided directly below the abstract. key words should express the precise content of the manuscript, as they are used for indexing purposes.

</td></tr>
</table>

<table>
<tr><td>

INTRODUCTION

- Maximum 3-4 paragraphs
- 100-200 words to introduce your topic
- 500-1000 words of literature review
- Last paragraph should be the aim of the study (general objective)

</td></tr>
</table>

<table>
<tr><td>

METHODS

- 200-400 words
- Describe study population and location
- Study design & Sampling methods
- List of questionnaires used and from where adopted?
- Any pretest done? Validation?
- State ethics approval from which institute
- Did all participants sign the consent form?

</td></tr>
</table>

RESULTS

- 500 – 1000 words
- No need to explain each table in detail, only headlines
- First paragraph describes the characteristics of the sample

DISCUSSION

- Maximum 3-4 paragraphs
- 500-1000 words
- 1ST paragraph the study main findings
- 2ND paragraph: the study limitations
- 3RD and 4th paragraph: compare your results with previous studies

CONCLUSION

- 200 words
- 1 paragraph
- Maximum 3-4 sentences

ACKNOWLEDGMENT

- 1 or 2 sentences

COMPETING OF INTEREST

- Authors need to declare if they have any competing of interest

REFERENCES

- Depend on each journal style

TABLES

- Maximum of 4-5 tables
- Title of each table must be self-explanatory
- Include confidence interval and p value where possible
- Table should not be large (maximum 6 columns and 12 rows)
- Table 1: Socio-demographic characteristics
- Table 2: Dependent variable (outcome)
- Table 3: Association table (Socio-demographic and dependent)
- Table 4: Association table (other factors and dependent)
- Table 5: Multivariable table

Verb Tense to use in writing research manuscript

❖ Abstract

<u>Past</u> to describe actual results

<u>Present</u> to tell facts or findings from analysis

❖ Introduction

<u>Present</u> to describe background

<u>Present perfect</u> to tell about previous

research

❖ Methods

<u>Past</u> to describe what you did

<u>Present</u> to explain diagrams or figures

❖ Results

<u>Past</u> to describe actual results

<u>Present</u> to explain tables or figures

❖ Discussion

<u>Past</u> to summarize findings

<u>Present</u> To interpret significance of findings

❖ Conclusion

Past to talk about completed research

Present to discuss implications and suggest future research.

- **References**

- Ghazi HF, Isa Z, Aljunid S, Shah SA, Tamil AM, Abdalqader M. The negative impact of living environment on intelligence quotient of primary school children in baghdad city, iraq: A cross-sectional study. BMC Public Health. 2012; 12:562.
- Hasanain Faisal Ghazi, Maged Elnajeh, Mohammed A. Abdalqader, Mohammed Faez Baobaid and Indang Ariati Ariffin, 2018. Non-communicable diseases and its association with body composition and nutrition among general population in Subnag Jaya, Selangor: community-based study. Pak. J. Nutr., 17: 255-259.

- Aniza Ismail, Hasanain Faisal Ghazi, Ismail M.S & Nurul'Ain A. Disaster management: identifying knowledge of emergency nurses and community health nurses and its predictors in malaysia. Malaysian Journal of Public Health Medicine 2016, Vol. 16 (3): 66-74

- https://www.scribendi.com/advice/reference_manage
  ment_software_solutions.en.html (accessed on 8th
  July 2019)